THE DIVINE VERDICT

God Has The Last Word

Fulton J. Sheen

Bishop Sheen Today
280 John Street
Midland, Ontario, Canada, L4R 2J5
www.bishopsheentoday.com

Library of Congress Cataloging-in-Publication Data
Names: Sheen, Fulton J. (Fulton John), 1895-1979, author. | Smith, Allan J., Editor.

Sheen, Fulton J. (Fulton John), 1895-1979. The Divine Verdict. Registered in the name of P.J. Kenedy & Sons under Library of Congress catalog card number: A 173970, following publication June 28, 1943.

Title: The Divine Verdict. God Has the Last Word. Fulton J. Sheen, author; edited by Allan J. Smith.

Description: Midland, Ontario: Bishop Sheen Today, 2023.

Includes bibliographical references.

Identifiers:
ISBN: 978-1-998229-11-6 (paperback)
ISBN: 978-1-998229-05-5 (e-book)
ISBN: 978-1-998229-13-0 (hardcover)

Subjects: Judgement – Freedom – Morality – Peace – Evil –

To Mary

**Immaculate Mother of God,
Gracious Queen of Christ's afflicted
ones, in prayerful petition
that the Glorious Peace of Christ
may reign in the souls of men.**

CONTENTS

INTRODUCTION.. 1

EVIL HAS ITS HOUR.................................... 9

WAR AS A JUDGMENT OF GOD 27

JUDGMENT OF NATIONS 45

FREEDOM IN DANGER............................. 59

MORAL BASIS OF PEACE 73

JEW AND CHRISTIAN 91

THE POWER OF GOD 105

ACKNOWLEDGMENTS........................... 117

ABOUT THE AUTHOR 121

INTRODUCTION

When looking back on the life of Archbishop Fulton J. Sheen, there are some that would refer to him as 'a man for all seasons'. Over his lifetime, he spent himself for souls, transforming lives with the clear teaching of the truths of Christ and His Church through his books, radio addresses, lectures, television series, and many newspaper columns.

Fulton J. Sheen was born in 1895 in El Paso, Illinois. He lived and studied through a time in history in which he witnessed the effects of two world wars and many social, political, and economic conflicts.

While a graduate student and university professor in the United States and Europe, Sheen made friends with a number of the great thinkers and writers of his day such as G.K. Chesterton, Christopher Dawson, J.R.R. Tolkien, and C.S. Lewis.

After his ordination to the priesthood in 1919, Sheen would go on to receive numerous degrees from the Catholic University of

America, Louvain University in Belgium, and the Angelicum University in Rome.

From 1926-1950 he was a full-time professor at the Catholic University of America, first in the School of Theology and later in the School of Philosophy. At the beginning of his teaching career, Sheen was regarded with esteem as one of the premier scholars of his time. The publication of his first book in 1925, *God and Intelligence in Modern Philosophy: A Critical Study in the Light of the Philosophy of Saint Thomas,* garnered Sheen extraordinary respect for his scholarship on St. Thomas Aquinas. The book was so well received that Sheen was awarded the Cardinal Mercier International Philosophy Award. Also impressed with the content was G.K. Chesterton, whose admiration is evidenced by his willingness to write the book's introduction.

During his time at the Catholic University of America, Sheen wrote thirty-four books on various topics. He also was the featured speaker on the Catholic Hour radio broadcast, having millions of listeners tuning in each week.

Witnessing the threat of Communism on the rise in the 1920s, it became sufficiently clear to Sheen that modern atheism was not only an esoteric philosophy preached by learned professors at Harvard and Yale, but it was a new type of Messianism emanating from Moscow, threatening to cover the face of the earth. So in the same year in which Pope Pius XI issued his encyclical on atheistic Communism (1937), Fulton J. Sheen published three books titled: *'Communism'*, *'Communism and Religion'*, and *'Liberty Under Communism'*.

Sheen stressed the need for the use of reason in dealing with Communism. On the subject matter, he was no intellectual featherweight, and he brought his formidable powers of intellect to bear on the problem of Communism, the better to refute it. He absorbed Marx, Lenin, and Stalin to prepare himself for the assaults he would sustain in his deconstruction of their theories. He was a tremendous success. He converted or influenced several Communists and leftists in the heyday of American Communism, including Louis Budenz, Elizabeth T. Bently, Bella Dodd, and Heywood Broun.

Toward the end of the 1930s, talk of war began to surface. When German forces invaded Poland on September 1, 1939, World War II began. Almost immediately Fulton J. Sheen rose to the occasion of being called to bring sense to a nation that was looking for answers to the questions of war. During his presentations on the radio he encouraged his audience to think of the great spiritual transformation that there would be in America if every Jew, Protestant, and Catholic according to the light of his conscience prayed one continuous hour a day, for the president, for Congress, and for victory.

Archbishop Sheen called World War II not only a political struggle, but also a 'theological one'. He referred to Hitler as an example of the "Anti-Christ." Sheen also said that, "the means of life no longer ministers to peace and order because we have perverted and forgotten the true ends of life... It is not our politics that has soured, nor our economics that have rusted; it is our hearts. We live and act as if God had never made us."

In 1941, the United States officially entered World War II. That same year Sheen penned the book *A Declaration of Dependence.* In it, Sheen writes, "The Declaration of Independence, I repeat, is a Declaration of Dependence! We are independent of dictators because we are dependent on God. God is the necessary factor of our salvation. As a result, he is to be the center of our lives. His ways ought to permeate every aspect and area of our lives: education, employment, pleasure, mourning, socializing, etc. All is done in sight of the omnipotent Lord, and all we do should be done reflecting this knowledge. Our every interaction should be filled with the love of our Savior."

Numerous articles, radio reflections, and books would continue to be produced by Sheen throughout the war. Given their importance and the impact they had on society in his day, it seemed appropriate to bring together once again some of Archbishop Sheen's reflections on war and peace taken from his book *The Divine Verdict* (New York: P.J. Kenedy and Sons, 1943)

Here you will a collection of Sheen's Catholic Hour radio addresses that were heard by millions of listeners each week. These reflections are a series of short essays that addressed the many concerns of the listeners of his day during the war.

Sheen answers questions about the moral basis of peace, the power of God, war being a judgement of God and the judgement of nations. Sheen also explains how evil Has Its Hour and how our freedoms are in danger.

His were some of the most clearly delineated investigations into the underlying causes of the war combined with an entirely sound and hopeful program for winning both the war and the even more important peace are found in them. These powerful reflections can be most heartily recommended for their wise counsel, sane and penetrating analysis, and logical conclusions.

Sheen writes, "There are two ways of looking at the war: one as a journalist, the other as a theologian. The journalist tells you what happens; the theologian not only why it happens, but also what matters. Our approach is from the divine point of view, first of all, because it is the only explanation which fits the facts; secondly, because the American people who have been confused by catchwords and slogans are seeking an inspiration for a total surrender of their great potentialities for sacrifice, both for God and country."

Sheen is firm in his conviction that real peace cannot be declared, it must be made. It is with peace-making and the fundamental conditions on which peace must be based that this book is concerned. In its seven forceful and readable chapters, it challenges the theory of many planners today who posture that military allies are necessarily political allies; it affirms that a common hatred can make nations allies, but only a common love can make them neighbors; it denies the primacy of action over reason, in the sense that the will of the state is that which makes a state right; and it contends that utility does not establish justice, but it is justice which makes utility.

With the same lucid and persuasive reasoning that has made him outstanding both as a writer and as a lecturer, Sheen continues to challenge people of goodwill to unite for the preservation of personal rights, freedom of conscience, human justice, and civilization itself – all of which are in danger in the present conflict. Here, one will recognize the urgency of Sheen's subject matter, and will find pillars of peace and promise in his far-sighted principles.

Archbishop Fulton J. Sheen's destiny was encrypted in his name, for in the Gaelic language *Fulton* means *war* and *Sheen* means *peace.* Sheen's lifelong goal was to establish peace, but in that call, he inevitably came up against many obstacles toward that noble ideal. It is as though his very name foretold the kind of life he was to have: an uninterrupted warring against the powers of darkness to promote the peace of Christ's kingdom.

EVIL HAS ITS HOUR

Perhaps there is no misunderstanding of religion more universal than the one which assumes that evil cannot be reconciled with God.

A war seemingly adds great weight to the difficulty, for in such tragic moments the scoffer asks: "Where is your God now?"

We are never asked to justify God in the days of prosperity, simply because so many think it the supreme business of God to make us prosperous.

As Aeschylus wrote five centuries before Christ: "A state that is prosperous always honors its gods."

As an Italian proverb has it: "In prosperous times no altars smoke."

But in days of adversity, those who retain their faith in God are asked to justify His existence. God, some think, should always be a success in the worldly sense of the term.

The thief on the left, for example, identified the goodness of God with His Power to remove him from the gibbet, that he might be restored to the ways of thievery: "If thou be Christ, save thyself and us!" (Luke 23:39)

The bystanders at the Cross mocked in like manner: "He saved others, himself he cannot save! If he is the King of Israel, let him come down now from the cross, and we will believe Him. He trusted in God; let him deliver him now, if he wants him; for he said, 'I am the Son of God.'" (Matt. 27:42, 43)

This grouping of prosperity with Divinity falsely assumes that evil in some way lies outside and beyond the power of God, and that its presence necessarily spells the defeat of God. Nowhere do we find warrant for this view in the Scriptures.

It is interesting to note that one of the very first and one of the last statements Our Lord made in His public life was a warning to men that they be not scandalized at His momentary defeat. At the very beginning He said: "Blessed is he that shall not be scandalized in Me." (Matt. 11:6) The night He went out into the Garden of Olives He predicted to His Apostles saying: "All of you shall be scandalized in Me this night."

Quoting this centuries-old prophecy concerning not only His surrender to evil forces, but also their disloyalty, He said: "I will smite the shepherd, and the sheep of the flock will be scattered." (Matt. 26:31)

Scandals are inevitable when God works through the human, and when Eternity operates in time!

God in the form of a Babe, is a scandal! God hanging on a cross in a tattering human form, is a scandal! God present under the form of Bread, is a scandal! God absolving from sin in the form of a man, is a scandal! God communicating His infallible truth through a man, is a scandal! God giving to man the power to bind and loose on earth and in heaven, is a scandal!

But His admonition is: "Blessed is he that shall not be scandalized in Me." (Matt. 11:6)

Is God not right in warning us not to be scandalized at His failures? Would God be God if He could use only the good?

The Good are His willing instruments, but shall not Divine Power be capable of using unwilling instruments for His purposes? Anyone can make use of the good.

It is not our position here to reconcile the existence of God with evil; for evil is due, as we know, to an abuse of God's gift of freedom. It is the price we have to pay for divorcing freedom from God.

Rather, we seek here to justify the startling thesis that God permits evil from time to time for the sake of a greater good, so that in the language of St. Paul: "Where sin abounded, grace did more abound." (Rom. 5:20)

For some salutary lessons for these darkened hours, let us accompany in our mind's eye the Savior into the Garden of Gethsemane.

Three companions went with Him, Peter, James, and John, whom He strengthened for this ordeal by revealing to them His glory on the Mount of the Transfiguration.

No one in God's kingdom is ever called to glory and honor, except for the sake of tremendous responsibilities.

Bidding them to watch and pray, He went as far away from them as a man could throw a stone — what a significant way to measure distance — and prayed to His Heavenly Father, pledging to drink the chalice of redemption to its very dregs in ratification of His Divine Will.

Pulling down upon Himself the burden of the world's sin, as if He Himself has been guilty of sin; thrusting into His hand every open deed of evil and every secret deed of shame, as if He Himself has committed them.

He breaks out into a bloody sweat, as the crimson drops like so many words write on the pages of earth the story of its greatest Love and its fondest Hope.

When He had prayed, He came back to His chosen three, and found them wrapped both in their cloaks and in sleep. In return for His Love Our Lord had asked but one small thing — that they fall not asleep. He bade them stay awake like sentries of earth and bade them pray like sentries of heaven.

Everything slept about them. The city with its white-washed walls sprawling over the hills, was asleep; in all the houses of all the cities of the world, men were sleeping.

Perhaps the only ones awake were a thief in ambush in the dark, or a fond mother at the bedside of her sick child, or a sophomoric youth over a cup of wine in a dimly lighted tavern, asking his fellows: "Does God exist?"

Why did the Apostles sleep? Men sleep when they are tired, but they never sleep when they are worried. These men slept, and for only one reason — because they were not conscious of the awfulness of the Hour.

They were prepared for external dangers, for Peter was sleeping with his sword. But they were not prepared against themselves.

One can be armed and still be asleep — armed because one fears his enemies, asleep because he is not worried about his sins. Danger is physical; evil is moral.

Are we in America like Peter? Do we think of our times solely in terms of a war? Do we think of the Nazis and the Japs as being our only enemies? If so, as Our Lord told Peter, the sword is enough! But suppose they are only symptoms of evil and sin; then will the sword be enough?

When we have defeated them on the field of battle, will we have defeated the godlessness from whose womb they come? Will we in reality be cutting off only the evil fruit, but not uprooting the evil root? Do we realize how evil the times are?

We will search history in vain to find any other ages than our own, when nations made

expediency the sole ground of justice, when
freedom was derided and denied, when truth
was made the slave of a nation, a race or a
class, when some dictators would extinguish
religion altogether, when others would poison
it.

This war is not against rival political
systems or nations, but between contrary
philosophies of life.

Man is at war with his brother on the
battlefields of the world, because man has first
warred with God on the battlefield of the soul.
This war involves suffering only because it
first involved sin.

We are well armed as Peter was, and if all
we had to defeat were the Nazis and the Japs,
our task would be easy and victory certain.

But suppose we are fighting a devil?
Suppose we are defending ourselves against
philosophies of life which, as the Holy Father
said of Nazism, Fascism, and Communism,
are intrinsically evil. Then let us ask
ourselves: Will the sword be enough?

If we think of war only as a physical
combat as Peter did, we need to be aroused as
he was by the Savior, who reminded him of
two other arms: "Watch and pray." Watch! Be

vigilant on the outside. Pray! Pray that you may be armed on the inside with the armor of God.

Taunting Peter's false confidence in the sword alone, Our Lord asked: "Could you not watch one hour with me?" (Matt. 26:40) In other words, "Peter, there are twenty three hours a day you may spend with your armaments. But can you not give one Hour to invoking divine aid and imploring divine forgiveness"?

But why watch and pray? Because in times of crisis, evil can be more awake than goodness. Evil never sleeps.

Across this hill comes the evil man — Judas is his name. He leads a band of soldiers, Sadducees, and Pharisees, bearing lanterns and torches and weapons.

Judas has already given to them a sign saying: "Whomsoever I shall kiss, that is he; lay hold on him and lead him away carefully." (Mark 14:44) Then throwing his arms about the neck of Jesus, he blistered His lips with a kiss.

That kiss was at once the first and most horrible sullying of those lips which had pronounced the most heavenly words ever heard on this mad earth of ours. The betrayal of holy things must always be prefaced by a mark of affection.

The kiss was the first use of the Trojan Horse in the history of Christianity! Oh! How religion must guard itself against those wicked influences which say they are friends of religion.

This was no surprise to the Master. The very day He announced the Eucharist, He made known that Judas would betray Him. A few hours ago, before He gave the Eucharist, He told Judas himself he would betray.

It was thus around His most solemn promise and His most noble gift that the betrayal centered. As St. John put it: "Jesus therefore knowing all things that should come upon him, went forth and said to them: Whom seek ye? They answered him: Jesus of Nazareth. Jesus saith to them: I am he." (John 18:4-5)

When he said this the whole cohort of them fell backwards to the ground. Some burst of majesty halted them — some flaming glory which surpasses our puny minds. It was another way of revealing that no man could take His life, but that He could lay it down Himself.

Giving them power to rise, He took no thought of Himself, but of His faithless friends: "If therefore you seek me, let these go their way." (John 18:8)

"And Jesus said to the chief priests, and magistrates of the temple and the ancients, that were come unto him: Are ye come out, as it were against a thief, with swords and clubs? When I was daily with you in the temple, you did not stretch forth your hands against me: but this is your hour, and the power of darkness." (Luke 22:52-53)

"Your Hour" — the Hour of betrayers, deceivers, and crucifiers. "Your Hour" — the Hour for evil to put out the Light of the World — for that is all it can do during that Hour.

The Hour of wolves for scattering the sheep and seizing the Shepherd! The Hour of Power and Might and swords and clubs wherein Innocence and Truth are beaten to the ground. The Hour of concentration camps, Gestapos, O.G.P.U.'s, the Hour of the raping of Poland, the Hour of sending a peace envoy with a kiss while preparing an attack!

"Your Hour" — not because your weapons are stronger, nor because you come armed to seize Me, but because in obedience to the Father's Will, I deliver Myself into your hands that evil having done its worst may be overcome by Goodness rising from the dead.

In clear unmistakable language, Our Divine Lord here tells us that God permits the evil which the rebellious hearts of men beget to have its brief holiday even at the expense of God Himself.

The ignorant think that a war creates difficulties for belief in God. And here the Godman says that the evil seed man has planted will bear fruit in our evil hour!

It is not God's goodness we should doubt. It is our own! Evil did not come from God. It came from our sin, our pride, our egotism. Therefore it will have its hour!

Are we not living at such a moment now in the world's history? Do not the times in which we live belong to Satan and the Power of Darkness, wherein Divine Law is ignored, sanctuaries polluted, family life trampled under the feet of false freedom, and children raised as if there were no Cross, no Savior, and no Divine Love?

But if evil has its hour, how meet it? Will the sword be enough? Peter thought so!

Profiting by the confusion of the guards Simon Peter came suddenly to himself from sleep, drew a sword and struck Malchus, the servant of the high priest. It must have been a poor blow for it smote only his right ear.

Action is so often used as a substitute for prayer. So many think that the way to conquer an enemy's evil heart is to cut off his ear.

Simon's blundering action was remedied by the last act of Divine surgery wrought by the Savior Who heals the wounds that overzealous people make on other's souls.

This untimely action was repudiated by Our Lord. Addressing Peter, He said: "Put up again thy sword into its place: for all that take the sword shall perish with the sword." (Matt. 26:52)

Why did Our Lord not take up the sword offered in His defense? Certainly not because by using it, He might be courting military defeat; for "Thinkest thou," He said to Peter, "that I cannot ask my father, and he will give me presently more than twelve legions of Angels"? (Matt. 26:53)

And did He not say to Pilate: "If My kingdom were of this world, my servants would certainly strive that I should not be delivered to the Jews: But now my kingdom is not from hence." (John 18:36)

His motive then in rejecting the sword was not because He would have been no match for His adversaries. He asserts that if He did take to the sword, He would win every victory swordsmanship could achieve. And yet, believing this, He still refuses to use the weapon!

A physical enemy can be conquered with the sword. But moral evil can be overcome only by a Cross. Armaments will defeat a foe, but arms alone cannot conquer evil; and that is why He refused the sword in the Evil Hour!

Apply this to the war. Are we fighting the Nazis or the Japs, or are we fighting Evil? If only the former, our guns and tanks will do the job: but if they and other Dictators and evil philosophies are the products of our pride and egotism, then our armaments offer no guarantee of victory.

Evil has the devil on its side and no military power on earth can defeat the devil!

How blind are those that say: What good will prayer do? That is what Pater thought as he slept alongside his armaments.

One might just as well ask: What good will courage do? What good will faith in righteousness do? What good will belief in the Four Freedoms do?

Do we realize that what our totalitarian enemies are out to destroy is not what we have, but the principles for which we stand — a belief in human freedom and the value of a man against the power of the State? The soldiers who came into the Garden that night did not want Peter, James, or John. They were let go. Caesar wanted only Christ.

Our enemies, who are more numerous than We believe, seek to destroy the last vestiges of Christian civilization, so that they might; in the language of Nietzsche, so transvaluate values that evil from now on might be regarded as good and good be regarded as evil.

This warning, then! Unless we realize the fact that we live in an evil hour and that that hour must be spent watching and praying, we may end by drawing the enemy out of the House of Western Civilization, while into that empty house which should have been filled by Godliness, seven devils worse than the first will come in and dwell there and the last state of civilization shall be worse than the first.

Not until we realize that sin is the greatest evil in the world, and that wars, revolutions, and sufferings are the effects of sin, will we begin to take the path that leads to peace.

If this tragedy of war will not arouse us to the reality of an evil Hour, then how shall we yearn for God's Day?

Maybe a Michael is needed again to arouse us to the peril of the Hour:

Michael, Michael: Michael of the Morning
Michael of the Army of the Lord
Stiffen thou the hand upon the still sword, Michael,
Folded and shut upon the sheathed sword, Michael,
Under the fulness of the white robes falling
Gird us with the secret of the sword.

When the world cracked because of a sneer in heaven
Leaving out of all time a scar upon the sky
Thou didst rise up against the Horror in the highest,
Dragging down the highest that looked down on the Most High:
Rending from the seventh heaven the hell of exaltation
Down the seven heavens till the dark seas burn:

Thou that in thunder threwest down the
Dragon
Knowest in what silence the Serpent can
return.

He that giveth peace unto us; not as the world
giveth:
He that giveth law unto us; not as the scribes:
Shall He be softened for the softening of the
cities
Patient in usury; delicate in bribes?
They that come to quiet us, saying the sword
is broken
Break men with famine, fetter them with gold,
Sell them as sheep; and He shall know the
selling
For He was more than murdered. He was sold.

Michael, Michael: Michael of the Mastering
Michael of the marching on the mountains of
the Lord,
Marshal the world and purge of rot and riot
Rule through the world till all the world be
quiet:
Only establish when the World is broken
What is unbroken is the Word.

G. K. CHESTERTON

WAR AS A JUDGMENT OF GOD

Too exclusively and too long has modern man looked on this war in terms of politics and economics, and too little has he thought of it in terms of theology, morality, and the providence of God.

How many ever think of God as the Lord of History and the King of Kings?

Do not a number think of God only as an optional extra to whom appeal may be made at the end of political speeches, but who actually is as irrelevant to world events as poetry is to the problem of unemployment.

It would be nice if the poor knew Shakespeare, and it would be nice if men knew and loved God, but both are often regarded only as stimuli of an impractical character.

Others feel that a belief in God can be sustained in days of prosperity, for it is the business of God to supply 'pie in the sky'; but in time of trouble they feel that God's plans are in some way thwarted and His goodness can hardly be justified.

The reason for this is to be found in the Liberal Christianity which thinks of God solely as a God of sentimental love — such love as a doting modern mother might have for her erring son who could do no wrong, and even when he did it, must needs be forgiven, for he did not mean it.

Liberal Christianity has too long assumed that it is the sole business of the Church to beat the drums for social reform and to dance to the tunes piped for it by the latest moods and passing mental fashions.

It ignores the fact that the God of Love is also the God of Justice and that His wrath is terrible, and it forgets that the Christ Who forgives sinners is also the Christ Who will judge all men according to their works — for if God were forgiving without being just why should there ever have been a Cross?

It is the God of Justice who needs to be preached today. Modern man's dictum — "Religion has nothing to give me" — has been too long unanswered. Now let the answer be given: Certainly, it can give him nothing; but it can take away something — it can take away his diabolical pride, your self-sufficiency, and thus make room for morality and peace.

Let us discount all political and economic considerations as secondary and look at this war solely from the point of view of Divine Justice.

We commonly speak of this war as a Crisis. Our English word crisis is taken from a Greek word which means *judgment*; and that is just what this war is — a *judgment* of God.

History does not, as the Liberals believed a few years ago, move in a line of ascending progress. Rather it moves forward through catastrophies.

History is a moment given to man to say "yea" or "nay" to his eternal destiny; it is also a sphere wherein society works out the full effects of its allegiance to or its severance from God.

In the life of every human being, there is a *particular judgment* and a *general judgment*.

The *particular judgment* comes at the moment of death, for we are individually responsible for the way we used our God-given liberty; the general judgment comes at the end of time, because we work out our salvation in the context of the social order and the brotherhood of Christ, and therefore we must be judged with the entire world.

History too, like individuals, has its particular and general judgments. Particular judgments come at various moments in a nation's history, when it works out the full moral consequences of its decisions and its philosophy of life. The General Judgment will be at the end of time when Our Lord shall come to judge all the nations of the world.

We find a reference to both the particular and the general judgments in history, in Our Blessed Lord's warning to the City of Jerusalem.

Because it had not known the time of its visitation, He said that a particular judgment would come before that very generation would have passed away, when the enemy would beat it flat to the ground. That judgment actually came to pass in the year 70 when Titus destroyed the Holy City.

But Our Dear Lord also foretold, in the same passage, the general judgment of the world in the distant future unknown to the sons of men, when nations which judged Him would then be judged by Him, as He would come in the clouds of heaven bearing His Cross in triumph.

By speaking of the two together, He seemed to suggest that particular judgments in history are merely rehearsals for the General Judgment when the decisions of free men shall be sealed for all eternity.

We are presently living in a moment of particular judgment on history. In other words, our present world crisis is a judgment of God on our era and our times.

But what is meant by the Judgment of God? We mean by it a "verdict of history." It is a time when the full consequences of our way of life become evident.

The Judgment of God definitely does not mean that God is *outside* history as a mighty Potentate Who occasionally, to remind subjects of His power, smites them for His good pleasure. Neither does it mean that this war is a divinely sent visitation or punishment, extrinsic and unrelated to our existence, as a spanking to a child who stole the jam — for a spanking does not *necessarily* follow the stealing.

The Judgment of God means that the Transcendent God is also inside History by His Laws, far more intimately than an inventor is in his machine, or an artist in his painting.

God has implanted certain laws in the universe by which things attain their proper perfection. These laws are principally of two kinds: natural laws and moral laws.

What we call the natural laws, such as the laws of astronomy and the laws of physics and the laws of biology, are in reality so many reflections of the Eternal Reason of God. God made things to act in a certain way. In this sense the oak is a judgment on the acorn; the harvest is the judgment on the seed that was sown.

But God did not make man like the sun which can only rise and set. Having made man free He gave him a higher law than the natural law, namely, the *moral law*. Fire must obey the natural law of its nature, but man merely *ought* to obey the moral law. His freedom gives him the license to rebel.

Now God's purpose in imposing law on things was to lead them necessarily to their perfection; and God's purpose in giving man the moral law was to lead him freely to his perfection.

To the extent that we obey God's will we are happy and at peace; to the extent that we freely disobey it, we hurt ourselves — and this consequence we call judgment.

Judgments are clear in the natural order. For example, a headache is a judgment on my refusal to eat, which is a law of nature; and atrophy of muscles is a judgment on my refusal to exercise.

So too there are judgments in the moral order "The wages of sin is death." (Rom. 6:23) "What things a man shall sow, those also shall he reap." (Gal. 6:8) "You ... have been called unto liberty; only make not liberty an occasion for the flesh." (Gal. 5:13) "By what things a man sinneth, by the same also he is tormented." (Wis. 11:17)

Disobedience to these laws entails certain consequences, not because we will those consequences, but because of the very nature of the reality which God *made*.

No one who over-drinks wills the headache, but he gets one; no man who sins wills frustration or loneliness of soul, but he feels it. In breaking a law we always suffer certain consequences which we never intended. God so made the world that certain effects follow certain causes.

When calamity comes upon us, as a consequence of our neglect or defiance of God's will, that is what we call the judgment of God. The world did not will this war, but it willed a way of life which produced it; and in that sense it is a judgment of God.

Sin brings adversity and adversity is the expression of God's condemnation of evil, the registering of Divine Judgment.

The frustration resulting from our disobedience to God's law is His Judgment. And in disobeying God's moral law, we do not destroy it — we only destroy ourselves. For example, I am free to break the law of gravitation; but in doing so, I kill myself — and the law still stands.

God therefore does not interfere with the world when it suffers Judgment, anymore than He interferes with it when we ruin our health by disobeying the laws of hygiene. He does not need to interfere, because He is already in the universe by His law.

The judgments of God are no more due to God's interference with the laws of nature than thunder is due to His interference.

God did not suddenly decide to applaud at the sight of pyrotechnics in the heavens. But He so made the universe that where there is lightning there is thunder. It is a certain effect following a certain cause.

Every now and then, we said, there are
particular judgments in history. Each era of
history is a field in which certain seeds are
planted. They grow, bloom, bear fruit, and die;
and the kind of ideas that are planted
determine the lot of that civilization.

The Religious Revolution was a judgment of
God on Christian people for not living up to
the full meaning of the Christian life. There
was nothing wrong with Christian dogmas, as
the Revolutionists assumed; there was only
something wrong with Christian morals.

The French Revolution was a judgment on
the selfish privileges of a monarchy and the
denial of political equality.

Communism was a judgment on Czarist
Russia and Capitalism; Nazism a judgment on
Versailles; and this war is a judgment on the
way the world thought and lived, married and
unmarried, bought and sold — a judgment on
the world's banks, its schools, its factories, its
homes, its legislatures, its international order,
its hearts and souls, and above all on its
humanist illusion that man could build a
peaceful world without God.

This war is to time what hell is to eternity
— the registering of the conflict of the human

will against the Divine. It was forged in exactly the same way as the Cross.

As the Cross was made by a horizontal bar of man crossing the vertical bar of God, so the war is the result of the contradiction of the Divine Will by the human.

The whole world stands under doom, because we are all guilty before God. Not all equally guilty, thank God, but guilty in vary. ing degrees.

We have not denied God as does Communism, nor have we set up a false god as does Nazism or Japanese Imperialism. But we have ignored God, or treated Him as a benignant power whose sole function it is to bless our plans, to sugar coat our idealism, and to lend a tone of respectability to a culture that is secularistic and man-centered.

The history of the world for the last few hundred years could be characterized as a progressive repudiation of the moral law and the gradual de-Christianization of society. This war, in other words, is a war within the human brotherhood because there has been a war against the Divine Fatherhood.

For centuries the foundation of our culture has been loosening; now the whole structure is collapsing. The world has completed the Grand Experiment of living without God! The world poisoned its own wells, and now blames God because the drink is bitter.

As hell is not sin, but the effect of sin, so this war is not sin — it is the wages of sin. We cannot war against God without warring against ourselves.

What is the purpose of Divine Judgments in history? They are guarantees of the permanence of the laws of God. Would men so universally respect the laws of health, if the violation of those laws did not entail such painful consequences?

Where would moral development be if fire burned today and froze tomorrow, if refusal to sleep strengthened us today and weakened us tomorrow, and if the moral law of God had consequences in the morning but not in the afternoon?

Judgment, or the consequence of our decisions, affirms that the world is informed by God's presence and is under His guidance. It is a reminder that God's moral law will never be destroyed, as the sun will never cease to rise in the east. He made the world that way.

In disobeying His Will, we destroy ourselves. In stabbing Him, it is our own heart we slay. By catastrophies must we sadly learn that the moral law is right and will prevail.

The judgment at the end of the world will be a guarantee of the eternal distinction between right and wrong. That is why there is a Heaven and a Hell; namely, because right is everlastingly right and wrong is everlastingly wrong.

The various judgments within history, such as this war, are guarantees of that distinction for the time in which we live. In plain simple language, the world which has blurred the distinction between right and wrong must be brought to the realization that "it cannot get away with it." It is a sign that we are on the wrong track.

Fire burns, therefore let us not stick our hands in it; Godlessness causes war, therefore let us be Godly.

All nations and all peoples must learn, in sorrow and tears and blood and sweat, that wrong attitudes toward the natural law and the moral law are simultaneously and necessarily a wrong attitude toward God, and therefore bring inevitable doom, which is the Judgment of God.

Up to this point we have spoken of the Judgment of God on the world. Now a word about that judgment in relation to our own beloved country. We have said that the terrible and awful consequences which follow a violation of God's law are reminders and guarantees that God's moral law is right.

As a nation we have never set up as a standard any other philosophy of life than the moral law. But we did permit the distinction between right and wrong to be blurred, particularly in education, where unprogressive teachers declared that the difference between right and wrong was only a question of a point of view.

It took a war to make education abandon that false notion, for no one now would say that the only difference between our cause and our enemy's was simply a matter of a point of view. In that sense, at least, this war is a Judgment of God on that false way of thinking.

The war has thus driven us back to a moral law outside ourselves, and, in fact, outside the world. For if the moral order for which we are fighting was of our *own* making, then why should not the Nazis say they had a right to fight for a moral law of their own making, that the only way to decide between the two would be by force and war.

If morality is national, there is no criterion except might. But suppose that the moral law for which we fight is not our own, but a derivative of the Eternal Reason of God. Then we fight not to decide which is the stronger, but rather to defend what is right.

This war is a Judgment! A Crisis! An effect of the repudiation of the moral law! And we are seeking to make the moral law prevail over the law of expediency and force.

We are fighting not for freedom from something, but freedom for something; namely, the right to develop personalities which are made to the image and likeness of God.

We are fighting not for the right of religious worship, for religion is not a right anymore than patriotism is a right. They are both duties. Patriotism is a duty to country; religion is a duty to God.

We are fighting not for any particular form of government, but for the right of all peoples to choose their own governments, which will exercise power with responsibility because that power comes from God alone.

We are fighting not for democracy, but for something deeper, namely, for the moral and religious foundations which make democracy possible.

We are fighting not because the Nazis and the Japs are devils, for how could there be devils unless there were fallen angels, and how could there be fallen angels unless there was a God against whom they freely rebelled?

Rather are we fighting to preserve a moral law of righteousness and justice, which we never realized was all-important until we saw its tragic and chaotic effects, but which now, with God's help, we will uphold, and in the name of which, with God's help, we will conquer.

A war could be the condition of world regeneration. Once before in history, on the hill of the Skull, three crosses with outspread beams, like giants with outstretched arms, silhouetted themselves against a sweet spring sky.

On the central Cross, hewn from a tree sown by a bountiful Creator, there now hung, by the perversity of man, Him Who made the flowers to bloom and the trees to grow. He had called men to holiness, and so He had fallen into the hands of unholy men and demons.

When finally He, unlike all other men, went out to meet death—for death did not come to Him, He bowed His head and died. His loud cry was so powerful that it rang around the earth and made the dead come from their graves.

A centurion who stood nearby — a typical sergeant in the great Roman Army, who thought little of God and then only the gods Mars and Jupiter ran a lance into the heart of the dead King. And as he did so, he exclaimed: "Indeed this is the Son of God." He had found faith in the very moment he was using this lance.

And may God grant that we in America, who thought of God so little in the days of false peace, may perchance find faith in these days of war, as did the centurion — and cry out in the joy of regeneration: "Have Thy way O Lord, it is best for me."

JUDGMENT OF NATIONS

War, it was said above, is a Judgment of God, not in the sense that God acts *outside* history, but *inside* history, not as a smiting of creatures in an arbitrary fashion, but as a catastrophic effect following the breaking of His moral law.

These catastrophies are the guarantees that God's Will will prevail. God asserts His Sovereignty by the judgments which follow the disobedience of His laws; without such judgments, there is no sovereignty — even in our earthly courts. The world stands under doom because it pronounced antagonism to the Gospel of Love.

History affords us many interesting examples of the Judgment of God. Here we shall mention two instances of how forgetfulness of God brought on the ruin of nations, namely Jerusalem and Rome, and then show how two great Americans expressed the same vision of Judgment in our national life.

First the Fall of Jerusalem. The Great Patriot Who loved the Holy City as His own, stood on a hill opposite, and looking down upon it wept at the consequences which He knew would inevitably follow from a refusal to submit to the truth of which their consciences had already been convinced.

Amidst the shedding of tears, He lamented: "Jerusalem ... how often would I have gathered together thy children, as the hen doth gather her chickens under her wings, and thou wouldst not?" (Matt. 23:37)

That is the heart of sin! "I would ... thou wouldst not." The human will set up against Divine Will.

"I would have gathered ..." One man? A carpenter? No man can gather a civilization. Only the Son of God can gather a whole people.

"Behold! Your house shall be left to you, desolate." (Matt. 23:38) "For the days shall come upon thee: and thy enemies shall cast a trench about thee, and compass thee round, and straiten thee on every side, and beat thee flat to the ground, and thy children who are in thee; and they shall not leave in thee a stone upon a stone, because thou hast not known the time of thy visitation." (Luke 19:43-44)

And it came to pass as foretold. That generation did not pass away until the

calamity happened. Vespasian, going to Rome
to become Emperor, gave the order to his son
Titus, on Easter day in the year 70 to lay
waste Jerusalem. The Temple was destroyed,
not a stone left upon a stone.

History was the stage on which Jerusalem
worked out the full effects of its severance
from the laws of God. The city had not known
the time of its visitation. "Unless the Lord
build the house, they labor in vain that build
it." (Ps. 126:1)

The second example of how forgetfulness
of God brought on the ruin of nations is the
Fall of Rome. During the winter of 57-58 A.D.
St. Paul addressed a letter to the Romans,
from the city of Corinth, telling them of a
judgment that awaited them because of their
sins:

"And thinkest thou this, Oman, that
judgest them who do such things, and dost
the same, that thou shalt escape the judgment
of God? ... Knowest thou not, that the
benignity of God leadeth thee to penance? But
according to thy hardness and impenitent
heart, thou treasurest up to thyself wrath,
against the day of wrath, and revelation of the
just judgment of God." (Rom. 2:3-5)

St. Peter writing from Rome about the very year of his death, sounded the same Warning: "Whose judgment now of a long time lingereth not, and their perdition slumbereth not ... shall perish in their own corruption, receiving the reward of *their* injustice." (2 Pet. 2:3, 12-13)

These two men foretold the judgment of Rome, because it had forgotten God. Years later, in the year 370, at the mouth of the Danube, of a great Visigoth family, was born Alaric. None could have foreseen either his importance in history or the fact that he would unconsciously inspire one of the greatest heroic works ever written, namely, *The City of God*, by St. Augustine.

Alaric himself was probably a Christian, but Baptism had not destroyed in him a warlike lust. On three occasions he made visits to Rome, the third time being on the fourth of August, 410. With horses darting like hawks, and moving battering rams like mountains, he forced the Salarian gate, allowing his soldiers, who were the scum of Europe, to put the metropolis of the earth to sack and to humble the giant of the nations of the world.

On the seventh of August, followed by a long train of carts laden with spoils, he set

forth from Rome proceeding to the conquest of
Africa. But before setting sail for Sicily, he was
overcome by sudden death.

His soldiers, in accordance with an old
Goth custom, turned aside the River Busento
from its course, that they might bury in its
bed the body of Alaric the Daring, who had
thrice violated the Eternal City.

The fall of that city was terrible. It terrified
the whole Empire. The superb palaces of the
patricians were invaded, plundered, and set
on fire by the drunken barbarians. Virgins,
Christian and pagan, were violated, except
those who fled into Church.

Not for eight hundred years, since the
taking of Rome by the Gauls in 387 B.C., had
the Capital of the Empire been invaded and
outraged by barbaric hordes. Her surprise
then was greater than her terror, and her
shame greater than her surprise.

St. Jerome, writing on the Scriptures in the
cave of Bethlehem, heard the news and wrote:
"At the news my speech failed me, and sobs
choked the words that I was dictating. She
had been captured ... the City by whom the
whole world had once been taken captive."

At the close of that century, the Holy Father, Gregory the Great, standing at the tombs of the Apostles Peter and Paul, preached this sermon affirming the truth of the words of these Apostles already quoted:

"Today, there is on every side death, on every side grief, on every side desolation, on every side we are smitten, on every side our cup is being filled with draughts of bitterness ... (on the other hand) these saints at whose tombs we are now standing lived in a world that was flourishing, yet they trampled upon its material prosperity with their spiritual contempt. In that world life was long, well-being was continuous, there was material wealth, there was a high birth-rate, there was the tranquility of lasting peace; and yet when that world was still so flourishing in itself, it had already withered in the hearts of these saints."

In other words, almost four centuries before Rome fell, Peter and Paul said it would, because it had forgotten God. Now Gregory, representative of the Church which has survived the fall of all civilization, says that these men of the Church knew it would fall — and they saw it when Rome was strong and mistress of the world. In their eyes the city had written its own sentence of death with its own godless hands.

In our own American history, too, we find a recognition of the Divine Judgment. When Thomas Jefferson wrote the Declaration of Independence he penned these lines: "All men are created equal." He made no exception: "*All men.*" But he kept slaves! And he knew it!

To his credit, it must be said that he introduced a law into the Virginia legislature in 1778, prohibiting the slave trade, though slavery continued in the State.

Recognizing, however, the inconsistency and knowing that the blood of some men was in his own time being spilled by other men because they were denied equality, he expressed his fear in these words: "I tremble at my country, when I replied that God is just and that His Injustice does not sleep forever." It was a language almost identical to that which Peter used against Rome.

And well might Jefferson be concerned, for any nation which spills blood, either its own or another's, will have its own poured forth in reparation. "He who takes the sword shall perish by the sword."

We know well when the injustice was righted and the judgment came, for one man was great enough to see in the Civil War, a manifestation of the Justice of God: Abraham Lincoln.

"It is the duty of nations as well as of men," he said, "to own their dependence upon the overruling power of God; to confess their sins and transgressions in humble sorrow, yet with assured hope that genuine repentance will lead to mercy and pardon; and to recognize the sublime truth announced in the Holy Scriptures and proven by all history that these nations only are blessed.

"And inasmuch as we know that by His divine law nations, like individuals, are subjected to punishments and chastisements in this world, may we not justly fear that the awful calamity of civil war which now desolates the land may be but a punishment inflicted upon us for our presumptuous sins, to the needful end of our national reformation as a whole people?

"We have been recipients of the choicest bounties of heaven. We have been preserved these many years in peace and prosperity. We have grown in numbers, wealth, and power as no other nation has ever grown; but we have forgotten God.

"We have forgotten the gracious hand that preserved us in peace, and multiplied and enriched and strengthened us; and we have vainly imagined, in the deceitfulness of our hearts, that all these blessings were produced by some superior virtue and wisdom of our own.

"Intoxicated with unbroken success, we have become too self-sufficient to feel the necessity of redeeming and preserving grace, too proud to pray to the God that made us.

"It behooves us, then, to humble ourselves before the offended Power to confess our national sins, and to pray for clemency and forgiveness."

Thus spoke Abraham Lincoln.

This is one of the greatest documents ever written by the pen of any American. To Jefferson goes the credit of writing our Declaration of Independence. To Lincoln goes the credit of writing our Declaration of Dependence. Jefferson declared we were independent from tyrants; Lincoln added, we are Independent on God. The ethical complement to our Bill of Rights, he told us, is our Bill of Duties.

If Lincoln could come back today, would he not remind us in the midst of this awful war that we are under the judgment of God, and that prayer and reparation for our national sins may well be the essential condition of victory?

"It does behoove us," as he said, "to humble ourselves before the offended Power." And why? Because we will have greater burdens in peace than we will have in war. We will need God's assistance to make effective in deed, the words of our Atlantic Charter!

We are on record in the Atlantic Charter as guaranteeing the freedom and integrity of small nations. The Atlantic Charter is a kind of political counterpart to the Sermon on the Mount, for it is a defense of the weak and the poor.

The day Our Blessed Lord preached that Sermon on the Mount, He prepared His own Crucifixion; but little do those who isolate the Beatitudes from the Cross understand that one is inseparable from the other.

He knew that the weak could not be defended except by bearing the slings and arrows of the strong, and that to speak for the poor was to invite a cross from the rich.

How then shall our Atlantic Charter, which defends the integrity of small nations, become effective except by bearing the opprobrium of the strong? How shall we liberate the oppressed, except by being smitten with the sword of the oppressor?

The day we wrote that Atlantic Charter we wrote in ink something that can be fulfilled only in blood. The Atlantic Charter can come into being only as the Sermon on the Mount — by enduring a Golgotha for a few hours from the powerful Caesars of the earth!

Lincoln saw that when he wrote his Proclamation for freedom of the Negro — and we must see it too as we proclaim the freedom of the children and nations of the world.

No human power is strong enough to overcome the temptation to compromise with the strong? Whence shall come our energy to resist except from Him Who went from the Mount of His defense of the poor, to the Mount of a Cross where the Beatitudes became the flesh and blood of the civilized world?

The word "God" was left out of the Atlantic Charter, but our President did not leave it out of his declaration of war, for he ended it with these words: "So help us God."

And all Americans who are one with him in this war trust that when the day of Victory dawns, we will begin to talk of peace with the same words: "So help us God!"

FREEDOM IN DANGER

To avoid the Judgment of God by catastrophe we must relearn the meaning of freedom and justice. Justice will be the subject of the next chapter. Here we contend that freedom is in danger.

A proof that we are in danger of losing freedom, is because everyone is talking about it. If you suddenly came into a country where everyone was talking about the health of the lungs, you would immediately conclude that a disastrous microbe was rampant.

In the last war everyone spoke about "making the world safe for democracy," and yet the world became so unsafe for democracy, that within twenty-one years democracy had to stumble into another war to preserve itself.

Now, we ought to be worried about freedom, simply because everyone is talking about it! Slaves talk most about freedom; the oppressed, most about justice; the hungry, most about food.

We are all agreed that the external threat to our freedom and the freedom of the world comes from the totalitarian states. There is no need to develop this thesis. They are Satan's vice-regents of tyranny, the anti-Christ's advance agents of adversity.

But our point is that the gravest threat to freedom comes from within; not from *within America alone*, but from within the hearts and souls of men throughout the world.

While the world is attempting to preserve freedom in the political order, it is surrendering it in those deeper realms upon which the political reposes.

Picture a group of men on a roof-top proclaiming in song and story the glories of an architecture, while below, saboteurs have already knocked out half the foundations of the house, and you have the picture of modern freedom.

Politicians in the upper stories are glorifying freedom, while false philosophy, false education, and so-called Liberal Christianity have knocked away its supports.

The philosophical foundation is being undermined by the modern tendency to give the primacy to *will* over *reason.* In reality, however, the *reason* determines the targets or the goal of life; the *will* shoots the arrows.

The Christian mind, continuing the best tradition of the ancient world, contended that first there must be the truth of *reason*; then there is the action of the will — first the *target*, then the *arrows*. The modern world turns it around; first there is the *action*, then the *rationalization* of the action.

The difference between the two is well expressed by St. John and Goethe. St. John wrote: "In the beginning was the Word. ... And the word was made flesh." (John 1:1, 14) In other words, first the idea, then the deed; first the dogma, then the morals; first the program, then the fulfillment.

Goethe reversed it because he reflected the world-spirit in which he lived: "In the beginning was the deed." First you do whatever you please, then you use reason to justify what you have done; first you seize Poland, then you appeal to law; first you bomb Pearl Harbor, then you give reasons for declaring war; first you use Power, then you find a Law to support it.

Now, modern philosophy and modern law, by making the will primary, have made reason its servant. But Will without Reason is Will to Power. Reason then has no other function than to justify its violence.

If we live without the goals and purposes of life, which reason gives us, and if we define freedom as the right to do whatever we please, then how can we decide between conflicting wills except by force and violence?

We are thus destroying freedom in our souls by bad thinking while we mouth it most loudly with our lips. We are in graver danger than we know.

Freedom is also denied in education today. This may sound bizarre to some educators who have been shouting catch-words about *freedom* for decades. But I submit they are talking about *license* — not *freedom*.

They are concerned with freedom *from* something; not freedom for something; they are interested only in freedom without law and discipline, rather than freedom within the law.

And the proof? Do not many educators today assume that evil and sin are due to ignorance, and that if we educate, we will remove evil? Do not others assume that evil is due to bad environment, bad teeth, or bad glands, and that an increase of material wealth will obliterate evil?

Can they not see that these assumptions destroy freedom; for if evil is the result of ignorance, and not the result of a perverse use of freedom, then Hitler is an ignoramus, but he is not a villain?

Can they not see that education without a proper philosophy of life can be made the servant of evil, as well as good? Have they not the vision to see that if evil and sin are to be attributed solely to external circumstances, then man is not free to do wrong? Then wrong is in our environment, but not in us.

Is it not inconsistent to praise a free man for choosing what is right, and at the same time, when he does wrong, deny that he is free?

The fact is that sin and its possibility in this world are the evidence of freedom — a freedom not used rightly for God's purpose, but freedom abused for man's selfish ends.

Deny sin and you deny freedom. Deny that man can do evil, and you deny that man can in this world freely do good! That kind of education is destroying freedom in our schools, while our soldiers are fighting for it on the battle-fronts of the world.

Modern religion has also denied freedom. Do not misunderstand! It preaches freedom. But here we are searching hearts, not lips.

Modern religion denies freedom because it denies hell. In a recent survey of ministers it was discovered that seventy-three percent did not believe in hell.

If there is no hell, why should there be a heaven? If there is no wrong, and hence no sin for which men might be punished, why should there be a heaven where they should be rewarded for their virtues? If there are statues erected to our heroes, why should there not be prisons for our traitors!

Whom do they think God is — a kind of grandmother who laughs off the wrong-doing of His children, as if there were no scales of Justice, and He were not the God of Righteousness?

This sugary, pale ersatz of Christianity has not only set at naught the very words of the Christ Whom they preach — the Christ Who on more than a dozen occasions said there was a hell. Hell is the eternal guarantee of human freedom. If God were to destroy hell, at that moment He would destroy human freedom.

So long as there is a hell, we know that He so respects human freedom, that He will not by Force or Power destroy even that free will which rises up against Him with an everlasting "I will not serve."

These are the reasons why we ought to fear for freedom in the modern world. We should fear for it externally, because of the chains the dictators would forge on the anvil of war. We should fear for it internally because of the chains that are tightening within the modern heart — chains forged by a philosophy which destroys freedom by denying reason, by an education which destroys it by denying sin, and by a religion which destroys it by denying hell.

Satan is thus destroying our freedom at the very moment he has let us believe that we are most free. He has succeeded in destroying our freedom by the very same temptations in which he failed in tempting Christ.

Our Lord based His Kingdom on Love and therefore on freedom, for Love is the essence of freedom, as force is its very negation.

Satan tried to tempt Our Lord from His Gospel of Love by offering three substitutes. In the first temptation, instead of winning souls through love, Satan suggested Christ buy them with bread, inasmuch as men are hungry.

In the second temptation, instead of winning souls through freedom and love, Satan suggested Christ win them by manifesting great Power over nature, such as throwing Himself from a temple tower unhurt.

In the third temptation, Satan suggested winning souls through politics. He unfurled before the mind's eye of the Savior all the kingdoms and empires and nations of the world, and in a frightening boast said: "All these will I give thee, if falling down thou wilt adore me." (Matt. 4:9)

Our Lord refused to surrender freedom. If souls would not love Him without the bribery of bread, without the exhibitionism of Power, and without selling himself to Caesar, He would still not force them. Freedom would endure through an eternal heaven and an eternal hell.

Satan is now back again in the world, and how he is succeeding in destroying freedom!

Souls are today selling themselves out for that bread which they call security; for the power which is now called Science and Progress; while others, in over a fifth of the world's surface, have bartered their freedom for a political system under the control of a dictator.

Dostoievsky, that Great Russian writer of the last century, was right when in a great flash of genius he warned that the denial of sin and hell in education and religion would end in a world Socialism where men would surrender freedom for a false security.

Making the new anti-Christ speak to Christ, he says: "Dost thou know that the ages will pass, and humanity will proclaim by the lips of their sages that there is no crime, and therefore no sin; there is only hunger?"

Finally with license, freedom and science without God, the anti-Christ tells Christ in the words of Dostoievsky that license will end in class conflict, hatred, and a surrender to an Omnipotent State in a vain attempt to correct these very evils:

"Freedom, free thought, and science, will lead them into such straits and will bring them face to face with such marvels and insoluble mysteries, that some of them, the fierce and rebellious, will destroy themselves, others, rebellious but weak, will destroy one another, while the rest, weak and unhappy, will crawl fawning to our feet and whine to us: 'Yes, you were right, you alone possess His mystery, and we come back to you, save us from ourselves!" (1)*

Finally, in place of free men, the anti-Christ pictures the new Socialistic State in which he and his followers will organize everything after convincing people there is no sin — there is only hunger.

"They will tremble impotently before our wrath, their minds will grow fearful, they will be quick to shed tears like women and children, but they will be just as ready at a sign from us to pass to laughter and rejoicing to happy mirth and childish song.

"Yes, we shall set them to work, but in their leisure hours we shall make their life like a child's game, with children's songs and innocent dance. Oh, we shall allow them even sin, they are weak and helpless, and they will love us like children because we allow them to sin.

"We shall tell them that every sin will be expiated, if it is done with our permission, that we allow them to sin because we love them, and the punishment for these sins we take upon ourselves. And we shall take it upon ourselves, and they will adore us as their Savior who have taken on themselves their sins before God. And they will have no secrets from us.

"We shall allow or forbid them to live with their wives and mistresses, to have or not to have children according to whether they have been obedient or disobedient — and they will submit to us gladly and cheerfully.

"The most painful secrets of their conscience, all, all they will bring to us, and we shall have an answer for all. And they will be glad to believe our answer, for it will save them from the great anxiety and terrible agony they endure at present in making a free decision for themselves."

And anti-Christ continues: "What I say to Thee will come to pass, and our dominion will be built up. I repeat, tomorrow Thou shalt see that obedient flock who at a sign from me will hasten to heap up the hot cinders about the pile on which I shall burn Thee for coming to hinder us. For if anyone has ever deserved our fires, it is Thou. Tomorrow I shall burn Thee." Dixi. (2)*

Where shall we go for a defender against this slavery of anti-Christ? Only to Him Who resisted and overcame him on the Mount of Temptation and on the Mount of Calvary.

On Calvary it was not only the ancient world, but our own world of today which challenged: "Come down and we will believe."

They were willing to admit that they would believe if He would only show His Power by stepping down from His gibbet!

Poor fools! Did they not see that they were asking Him to force them to believe, which would have been the end of freedom? They were free to believe that He was the son of God, as the thief said, so long as He did not come down to smite them!

They had freedom so long as He left their faith in their own hands and not in His. His refusal to come down was the battle flag of freedom. The nails which pierced Him were the stars of the flag of freedom; the bruises of His body battered by free men, were the stripes of that flag. His blood was its red; His flesh its blue and its white.

So long as Our Lord hangs on His Cross, man is free! The moment He comes down in Power, man is His slave, and He is man's dictator. But come down He will not! Freedom will never be destroyed. Not even in hell will He dictate, for even man has the eternal choice of his rebellious will.

So He did not come down! Because it is human to come down! If He came down He would have made Nazism, Fascism, and Communism before their time. The coming down is the death of love. If He came down, He never would have saved us! It is divine to hang there!

Unfurl and wave to the four winds of the world, "O battle flag of Freedom." There will always be freedom when men are not forced to love; but there will always be love when we are not forced to be free!

(1) * Dostoievsky, The Brothers Karamazov, p. 268, Tr. Constance Garnett. Modern Library Edition
(2) * Dostoievsky, Ibid., pp. 269-270.

MORAL BASIS OF PEACE

All our talk about spheres of influence, global strategy, Balkan Federations, international courts, Beveridge plans, freedom and democracy, will collapse like a house of cards unless based on the moral order of Justice. As Pius XI said:

"To create the atmosphere of lasting peace neither peace treaties nor the most solemn pacts, nor international meetings or conferences, nor even the most disinterested efforts of any statesmen, will be enough, unless in the first place are recognized the sacred rights of natural and divine law." (Pius XI, 1931.)

In other words a strong sword can put an end to the war, but it cannot beget peace; for peace does not come from the womb of arrested hostilities, but from Justice rooted in God.

Families who are quarreling over a back fence may stop fighting when one of them runs out of bricks, but peace will not follow unless a change takes place in their hearts.

Perhaps then this talk may not be so impractical after all. Maybe the world is in this mess simply because our world is controlled by men who are too impractical.

When a machine is half out of order any tinker can fix it, but when it is completely broken down it calls for the attention of the expert. Practical men are always trying to build a Bethlehem of peace and glory and angel songs with the modern counterparts of gold, frankincense, and myrrh — namely, money, chemistry, and death-dealing armaments, but they never think of the Babe.

These practical planners who think that all the conditions of peace are within the domain of politics, economics, and finance are going to end like a man who might add two and two together and get the surprise of his life. They assume that the international order is a great machine which will run perfectly if it is efficiently planned and oiled from the international vats of good will.

But the tragic fact is the international order is more like a living organism composed of human beings with their own wills and springs of actions, and hence the functioning of the organism depends on the thoughts they think, the law they obey, and the justice they serve.

In order to bring home the importance of a moral basis for peace, we ask these questions: Why should any of the treaties or pacts signed at the close of this world war be kept? What guarantee have we that they will be honored more from 1943 to 1963 than they were in that twilight of honor from 1918 to 1939?

What right have these journalists and educators who have been sniping at the moral law for decades, to expect that the honor born of morality — which they impugn — will be the unbreakable code of international affairs?

What promises can we trust, in what agreement can we confide, what treaty is not a scrap of paper, if pragmatic education, now called "realist," assures us that the absolute distinction between right and wrong is not grounded in Eternal Justice, but is a relic of primitive taboos and a hangover from medieval blindness?

No one ever seems to discuss this question: But it is so elementary that until we answer it there is no reason for making any treaties.

One reason given for the keeping of treaties is based on custom, but what makes the custom? And is it not more customary to break treaties today than to keep them? As

Shakespeare might say: "a custom honored more in the breach than in the observance."

Another reason given is that treaties bind because nations freely enter into them. But what is to prevent nations from freely walking out on treaties, as Russia and Germany did in the case of Poland, and Japan did in the case of China, and Italy did in the case of Ethiopia?

A third reason, which is the Pragmatist or Positivist theory of law, and which is most common today even among our own jurists, is that a treaty is binding because it is advantageous or expedient to have it so.

But suppose it ceases to be advantageous, or suppose it becomes more expedient to abandon it — Alas! Hitlerism! Pragmatism is the philosophy which holds that the true is the useful, and certainly nothing could be more useful today than to be something more than a Pragmatist.

As Longfellow once said: "Morality without religion is only a kind of dead reckoning — an endeavor to find our place on a cloudy sea by measuring the distance we have run, but without any observation of the heavenly bodies."

When one gets down to rock bottom, there are only two possible reasons for keeping treaties; either because of force, or because of moral obligation. If force, then Might makes Right; then the Nazis are right in Holland and Belgium, and the Japs are right in the Philippines; then if the Nazis and Japs conquered us, which God forbid, the treaties they would make would be just because imposed by force.

The theory of force sees right when we can apply the force, but in itself force can never make right. Force works on brutes, it does not work on men.

Power without morality is power without responsibility. As Lord Acton said: "Power corrupts, and absolute power corrupts absolutely."

And shall we who live in the tradition of the Declaration of Independence forget that the pursuit of happiness is not down the road of the pursuit of power. As Thomas Jefferson said: "I have never been able to conceive how any rational being could propose happiness to himself, from the exercise of power over others."

Beware of power. It is more dangerous now than ever, for power is today passing again from the many to the few. It used to dwell in the masses; now it is enthroned in dictators.

Like other Pilates they still say to Innocence and Truth and Justice: "Knowest thou not that I have power to crucify thee?" (John 19:10) Shall we who boast we are defending the Christian cause, forget that against all who would make Power the seed of Justice, the Master said: "Thou shouldst not have any power against me, unless it were given thee from above." (John 19:11)

Outside Power-force there is only one reason for keeping treaties, namely, because a treaty imposes a moral obligation rather than a physical one. A treaty is a sacred thing because the God of Justice is its witness.

That is why certain things are eternally right and others eternally wrong. And in its general outlines, there is no difference between Christian morality and pagan morality, for God is the source of both.

Christianity did not impose a set of moral sentiments on the world of which the world never heard before; and the pagans would never have accepted the supernatural standards of morality if they had not already found a response in the natural standards of morality already written on the tablets of their hearts.

That is why there runs through history a record of sacredness of treaties based on the moral order. The Jews made their treaties "in the name of the Lord God of Israel." Almost all the nations of antiquity surrounded their treaties with religious symbols and rites.

Horace expressing the best of the Roman tradition warned: "What profit vain laws without moral support."

Lincoln in his first Inaugural Address, expressed the American tradition by reminding himself that his oath was registered in heaven: "You can have no oath registered in heaven to destroy the government; while I shall have the most solemn one to preserve, protect and defend it."

And Benjamin Franklin, in November, 1728, expressed the idea that a word ought to be kept, not because it is prudent policy, but because we are children of God and under His moral law: "That I may have a constant regard to honor and that I may possess a perfect innocence and a good conscience, and at length become truly virtuous and magnanimous — help me, good God; help me, O Father."

And all the treaties of Christian Europe from the very beginning were written in the spirit of an obligation rooted in morality, for they all began: "In the name of the Holy and Undivided Trinity." So they continued until the Treaty of Versailles, which began "In the name of the High Contracting Parties." Men had become "wise."

In the meantime they learned that man came from a monkey, that progress was due to evolution, that evil was due to bad glands, that morality was convention, and that God, in the language of a professor from Ohio, was "a projection into the roaring loom of time of a unified complex of psychical values."

And we wonder why we should have a second world war in twenty-one years?

Are we blind? Can we not see that if law is divorced from morality and religion, then treaties cease to be obligatory and begin to be mere arrangements, binding only so long as they are advantageous? Rob international justice of its roots in morality and treaties are hypothetical, not categorical; convenient tools, not honorable obligations, while law becomes an attorney's cloak woven from the Alimsy fabric of legalistic phraseology artfully placed on the shoulders of arbitrary power.

No wonder we had 4,568 treaties signed before the League of Nations from 1920 to 1939 and 211 signed the eleven months before the war.

Cowper described the result:

And hast thou sworn on every slight pretense
Till perjuries are common as bad pence;
While thousands careless of the damning sin
Kiss the book outside, who ne'er look within.

What difference does morality make in the international society? The same difference it makes in domestic society. When Catholics enter into a marriage pact, they know it is binding; they stake their eternal salvation on its timeless character; and they acknowledge that they should live up to its terms even when it goes against them. "Till death do them part" means "till death do them part."

But our modern pagans who have left religion behind do not scruple to make a marriage a pact terminable at the fancy of either party. Now international treaties grounded on morality are like marriages between Catholics, in the sense that honor is inseparable from morality; but international treaties without a basis in the moral law make orphan nations as divorces make orphan children.

A recent decision of the United States Supreme Court required one state to honor divorces of its own citizens obtained in another state with a six weeks divorce law, even though the divorcees went to the latter state merely to escape the greater severity of its own laws. I wonder if the advocates of such a system would agree that the treaties we make with Germany and Japan should be breakable at the end of six months on the ground of mutual incompatibility!

We cannot build up a stable, international society and pass peace on to the next generation until we lay to heart the basic conditions of peace: "Seek ye first the kingdom of God and his justice, and all these things shall be added unto you." (Luke 12:31)

Two impractical corollaries follow from the impractical principle:

First, the new League of Nations, or whatever it is called, should not be open to everyone, but should have membership in it conditioned upon the acceptance of certain basic moral principles of Justice. It should be more like a club than a street car; that is, it should have certain standards of admission.

The subscription rate of the last league was too low. Because anyone could walk in, anyone could walk out. Hence a nation or a state that will not accept a common ethos or set of moral principles, as superior to the sovereignty of any nation and existing before any nation began, and binding even when its application goes against itself, should not be permitted to sit in that august body, any more than a foreigner may sit in the councils of the United States.

Hence if a big nation makes a condition that it will not enter the League unless it can swallow up half a dozen small nations then let that power, whether it be Japan, Germany, Italy, Great Britain, Russia, or the United States, be quarantined until it recovers its ethical health. No court of justice can survive if the thief agrees to its decision only on condition that he can keep his loot.

Another corollary from the impractical principle that peace is inseparable from Divine Justice has to do with domestic society.

The loss of repentance in the spiritual order is paralleled by a loss of discipline in the social order. The very moment the Liberal theologians denied hell, which is one aspect of Divine Justice, educators denied discipline. Since there was no Divine Justice which had to be restored by repentance, so neither was there a social justice which had to be righted by appropriate penalties.

It was exactly the same mentality that produced Hitlerism in the international society and which produced hoodlumism and violent juvenile delinquency in domestic society.

Once Hitler found that he could seize the territory of other nations and trample on human lives with impunity because there was no vindictive justice, so in our large cities, individuals felt they could play fast and loose with property and human lives.

F.B.I. Chief, Mr. J. Edgar Hoover, reported to the House Appropriations Committee that prostitution by girls under twenty one had increased 64.8 percent over last year; that sex crimes by girls had increased 104.7 percent; that assault by males under twenty-one had increased 17 percent and rape 10.1 percent — that in spite of the fact that many young men are in military service. "Practically all these are civilian arrests."

Commenting upon it, he said: "If, during these trying periods we forget the moral needs of the next generation, we have not fulfilled the trust placed in us."

We found out that the only way to stop
international brigandage was by going to war
to restore justice; and we have yet to learn
that lesson in civil society.

Pupils who know they can insult their
teachers and escape punishment; youths who
know they can injure others without
themselves feeling a pain; delinquents who
know they can destroy property and then on
trial, as in one instance, be given candy by a
sentimental judge, or else have their evil called
"a fall in evolution" by a fuzzy social worker,
will go on and on disrupting the social order
as Hitler did, until they feel a few hard blows
of justice. There is nothing either in our social
system or in our educational system that
cannot be cured by discipline and the
restoration of justice.

Thus the denial of Divine Justice with hell
as the penalty for its repudiation inevitably
implies the denial of human justice with
discipline as the penalty for its violation. A
reprimand or a fine is no cure for a man
arrested for violence to his fellowman. There is
only one language such men can understand,
as there is only one language even Christians
can understand when we break God's law —
there is a hell!

Is there hope for the restoration of a moral order based on Justice! There is! Mr. Churchill last week told England that the nation's education must return to religion and morality — or perish. Mr. Roosevelt too said: "We are especially conscious of the Divine Power. It is seeming that at a time like this we should pray to Almighty God for His blessing on our country and for the establishment of a just and permanent peace among all the nations of the world."

There is hope too in the new America that is being forged on the anvil of war with the hammers of a Divine Justice. Most of the young men in our armed service are getting a sounder education than if they stayed in school, for they are now learning that the difference between right and wrong is so hard and so absolute that it takes death sometimes to make the right prevail. Their thinking has broken with our gilded past.

Some marines at Guadalcanal, looking at a few moronic, pathological youths bedecked in those glorified diapers called "zoot suits," said: "Maybe we ought to go back and clean up America."

Another wounded boy just back from the Pacific said: "Before I went to war, I believed that Justice was what I wanted; now I have learned to live and to fight for others."

And one need hardly recall the words of the soldier at Bataan: "There are no atheists in fox holes."

These boys are learning Justice the hard way, and they will love America even more when they come back.

For a parallel look to the American Legion of the last war, which more than any other organization in the United States — outside of the Catholic Church — consistently and fearlessly opposed the growth of Communism in our midst, which opposition within the past few days found its echo in the statement of the Attorney General of the United States: "It may not be good for Russia to get rid of the Communists, but it will be good for America."

These boys of ours in like manner will know the wrong things and the right things when they come back, for they are now finding them out in the mud of Africa, on the rolling seas of the Atlantic and the Pacific, in the jungles of New Guinea and the swamps of the Solomons.

When we go out to work, we know we will come back; when they go on the field, in the air, or on the sea, they have a rendezvous with uncertainty and they seem to care less because they have one supreme interest — the taking of the "objective." And all morality is grounded on an objective on an end, a goal — on God.

We will have an invasion when this war is over — not from a foreign enemy, but an invasion of great men, twice-born Americans. And unless we get down on our knees and transform our hearts by prayer as they have by sacrifice, we will not even understand the language they speak. Their values will be different; their outlook on life will be different. They will be the new America!

And those who do return will never be able to blot out of their memory the thousands of little white crosses they left behind marking a spot where foreign earth is piled high on hearts that loved American soil.

Those crosses will be symbols of the Justice for which they fought, vertically pointing up to God from whom Justice is derived, and horizontally pointing outward to America to whom that Justice will be applied. Each little white cross will be as a miniature Calvary and cameo Golgotha, and as a splinter from a Great Cross whence comes "Greater love than this no man hath."

And when finally the taps sound on the first night when the guns of the world go to sleep, we will join with them in beloved memory to those little white crosses and we shall pledge with them, that America shall have a rebirth of Justice under God, thanks to our martyred dead who have given to the earth some of the noblest red blood this earth of ours has drunk since Calvary drank the blood of Christ.

JEW AND CHRISTIAN

The two greatest vocations ever given to any peoples by God were given to Jews and Christians. The vocation of the Jew was the "giving of the Law, and the service of God and the promises." (Rom. 9:4)

Beyond all the ties of flesh and blood, and transcendent to membership in the same ethico-historical community, was the great supra-historical mission to be a chosen people selected by God, to be the vehicle of His Revelation to men.

The vocation of the Christian was to establish the brotherhood of men under the Fatherhood of God in the unity of the Spirit: "one body, one Spirit. ... One Lord, one faith, one baptism." (Eph. 4:4-5)

Not because of a common ethic, nor because they shared a vague admiration for a great humanitarian, but because of fellowship founded on the merits of Jesus Christ, the Christians have the supra-historical mission of proclaiming a fraternity of all men under the Kingship of Christ.

We must not allow individual defections from this unity to blur the picture. Whether individual Jews ignore the God of their fathers, or whether individual Christians live as if Christ had never died for their sins, does not alter the fact that there is in each instance a communal vocation, a divine mission entrusted to a people and to a kingdom.

The relation between the Jew and the Christian, from the Christian point of view, is the relation of father to son, of roots to branches.

In the magnificently strong language of Pius XI, who —commenting upon the words of the Canon of the Mass, *sacrificium Patri archae nostri Abrahae*, the sacrifice of our Father Abraham —said: "Notice that Abraham is called our patriarch, our ancestor. Anti-Semitism is incompatible with the thought and the supreme quality expressed in this text; it is a movement in which we Christians can have no part whatsoever ... anti-Semitism is unacceptable. ... Spiritually, we are Semites."

The Jew was given the vocation to be the chosen people announcing the law of God. The Christian was given the vocation of establishing the brotherhood of men in the Fatherhood of God, through the merits of

Jesus Christ. That brings us to this question: Have the Jews and Christians been faithful to their vocations?

First the Jews. There is a vast number who still are a devout, God-fearing, and God-loving people, but the spiritual condition of many Jews throughout the world today is sad — I say spiritual condition, for that is even more serious than their political condition. Very distinguished rabbis have told me that only one out of ten Jews attend a synagogue, either liberal or orthodox.

Some of their most distinguished fellows have repudiated all connection between Judaism and God.

Ludwig Lewisohn, well known in the Zionist movement, says "the Jew need believe nothing to be a Jew"; and Albert Einstein proclaims disbelief in a personal God, paying homage to a "cosmic religion" rather than to the God of Abraham, Isaac, and Jacob. Louis D. Brandeis confessed that "he had never gone to a synagogue."

To all who have the interests of God and immortal souls at heart, this condition is regrettable. It once awakened in the heart of St. Paul a great regret: "I lie not; my conscience bearing me witness in the Holy

Ghost: That I have great sadness and continual sorrow in my heart. For I wished myself to be an anathema from Christ, for my brethren, who are my kinsmen according to the flesh." (Rom. 9:1-3)

On the other hand, how many Christians are living up to their vocation?

A survey made by a Professor of Northwestern University into the belief of seven hundred ministers in and around Chicago representing twenty denominations revealed that 43 percent disbelieved in the inspiration of Sacred Scripture, though four hundred years ago that was their basic article of faith; 51 percent disbelieved in the necessity of Baptism.

And among the theological students who are today in the pulpit, the results were more staggering still: 69 percent disbelieved in the resurrection of the body; 52 percent denied that Christ would come again to judge the living and the dead; 61 percent denied the redemption of Christ on the Cross; and 37 percent denied the Divinity of Christ.

Suppose the same proportion of Americans disbelieved in the first ten amendments to the Constitution of the United

States. What would be the condition of democracy!

How many so-called Christians in the United States can recall the Third Commandment, and how many join with their fellowman in the worship of God?

This mass defection of Christians from Christ is tragic and it grieves the heart of all good Protestants who, with Catholics, confess Christ to be the Son of the Living God.

The fact is that both Jews and Christians are failing in their vocation: the Jews are failing in their vocation to be the people chosen to propagate God's Law, and the Christians failing in their vocation to preserve the brotherhood of men under the Headship of Christ.

This may not seem disastrous to a man without faith — but that is because the man without faith can see disaster only when it happens, never before it happens.

In order to bring home the awful consequences of this vocation failure among Jews and Christians, look to its social effects in the contemporary world. Before our very eyes there is being fulfilled the terrible warning: "The kingdom of God shall be taken from you." (Matt. 21:43) And so it has! By the Nazis and by the Communists.

Hitler, in so many words, says to the Jews: "You have had a vocation: the vocation to announce and to preserve the knowledge of the law of God, and to await as a chosen people the fulfillment of the promise given to you by God. But you have either forgotten it, or abandoned it.

"So I shall take the empty shell of your past, created by your own apostasy, and I shall further empty it of its Divine content: I shall prostitute and further secularize and profane it.

"I shall substitute the idea of the German race in place of the race of God, and the German Mission in place of the Divine Mission. This shall be the Messiahism of the twentieth century."

Communism says to the Christians: "You spiritual heirs of the Jews, who thought you also had an additional vocation—the vocation to preserve the brotherhood of men under the Fatherhood of God and under the Headship of His Son Jesus Christ — you have repudiated your Christ, your need of Redemption, your oneness in the Spirit. You have failed this supposed vocation and it has failed you.

"But we shall take it up, empty it of its Christian content, desecrate it, pervert it, harden it, and substitute the comradeship of violence for the brotherhood of love, and unite society on the basis of class hatred instead of the universal love of man in Christ. And this shall be the new brotherhood of the twentieth century."

Just as the French Revolution once prostituted the altar of Notre Dame by enthroning on it a courtesan as the Goddess of Reason, so now these new pseudo-religions and false mysticisms empty the people of God of God, and the brotherhood of Christ of Christ, and give to the world its anti-Semitic and anti-Christian Nazism and Communism.

As we supplied the Japs with steel which they converted into bullets to turn against us, so too have Nazism and Communism melted down the steel of two great vocations and made them instruments of persecution, of slavery, and of world disorder.

The chaos of the world is due in great measure to our failure to live up to the full responsibilities of our vocation. Neither of us has been all he was destined to be; we have failed in what God wanted us to be. "These things you ought to have done, and not to leave those undone." (Matt. 23:23)

A vocation to bear witness to God and a vocation to bear witness to Christ, like fine gold, have been melted down and an alloy substituted to make a base counterfeit. The very ideas that were meant to be channels for the salvation of souls have become sewers for the pollution of the world.

But they would not have so overflowed modern history if we, Jews and Christians, had been faithful unto the mission given us by God.

Nazism and Communism in a certain sense are a punishment on the Jews for failing to be faithful Jews and on the Christians for failing to be faithful Christians.

Both of them have forgotten the rock from which they were hewn, the fountain of living waters from which they sprang; and both have provided the instruments of the world's apostasy.

For that reason Nazism and Communism are in their essence not the resurrection of primitive barbarisms; they are worse — they are perversions of the spirit due to abandonment of faith in God.

Jews and Christians alike are being persecuted by the very ideas they either rejected or forgot. Never before in the history of the world has there been such a persecution of Jews and Christians.

There is as much anti-Semitism as there is anti-Christianity, and there is as much hatred of the Christians as there is hatred of the Jews. This should be to us a sign that we have entered into an apocalyptic period of history.

Drinking as we are, from a common chalice of misery, means that we have a common destiny.

In this new era of the world into which we are entering, there will be no persecution of one without the other. We are and will continue to be persecuted together, because the new spirit of the world is not non-religious, or indifferent to religion, or secularist, or humanist — it is anti-God. That means that all those who have any relation with God in their collective capacity will be persecuted.

To Nazism and to communism the Jews and Christians alike are demons. If the world hates the Jews and hates the Christians, it is because by vocation they are both "Outsiders" to the spirit of anti-God, regardless of how many faithless Jews or faithless Christians join their ranks.

There is a natural "divine discontent" in anyone who has a mission from God. Whether he be faithful to that mission or not, does not alter the fact. The anti-God world hates us because we have been God-summoned, and that is sufficient to inspire a persecution.

The Jews and Christians both possess a revolutionary character; they are in the world but not of it. Since God gave them a work to do, they are both alien, a ferment, a leaven forever disturbing the slumber of an anti-religious world.

That anti-God world will be touched neither by the finger of Abraham nor the finger of Christ, neither by the historical mission of Israel in time, nor by the healing mission of the Cross for eternity. It will, as the new City of Man, make war against the City of God until the consummation of the world.

It has stolen our thunder and now we must shrink in fear from its bolts.

In the name of God therefore let the Jews stop talking about anti-Semitic persecutions and the Christians stop talking about anti-Christian persecutions, as if a tree could be cut down without affecting both root and branch.

Opposition to the persecution of the Jews is and ought to be a Christian cause, as it is in Paris where the Catholic Auxiliary Bishop wears the five-pointed star of David on his sleeve. Opposition to the persecution of the Christians is and ought to be a Jewish cause as it is with some Dutch Jews who make their defence synonymous with Christianity.

The solution to the problem of the persecution of Jews and Christians is therefore not along lines of good fellowship, so-called tolerance meetings, or social unities which never mention religion.

Rather does the solution lie in these great vocations snatching back from Nazism and Communism the ideas of a chosen people and the brotherhood of man and infusing them once again with the Spirit of God, unto the regeneration of a world already reeling on the abyss of great disaster.

Let the Jews go back into their glorious history and relearn the words "Salvation is of the Jews." (John 4:22) What more glorious mission could one have than to be God's instrument of salvation?

Re-read your Jeremias! Renew a sense of your vocation: "But this shall be the covenant that I will make with the house of Israel, after those days, saith the Lord: I will write it in their heart: and I will be their God, and they shall be my people." (Jer. 31:33)

Open your Scriptures, ye Christians, and read the injunctions to walk worthy of your vocation to "press towards the mark, to the prize of the supernal vocation of God in Christ Jesus." (Phil. 3:14) "For if we be dead with him, we shall live also with him. If we suffer, we shall also reign with him." (2 Tim. 2:11-12)

Take back from Nazism the idea of the elect of God; steal back from Communism the idea of the brotherhood of man; revitalize them with the natural law and Divine Revelation and build a new and a decent world where a Jew and a Christian can live together in a world of God's righteousness and peace.

We are being driven together by the antiGod forces of the world. Hence the Jew will look in vain for peace in a secularized Messiahism or a Kingdom of God in some distant future here below. And the Christian will find only chaos in a humanism that attempts to make men brothers without a common Father.

Flimsy, indeed, is the unity of Jews and Christians which is based only on the hatred

of a common enemy. Strong will it be the day
we ground it on prayers to a common God.

This imaginative parable will illustrate our
meaning. Picture the Nazis desecrating a
Christian Church, turning it into a kind of
temporary Hall of Nazi Justice. Hitler walks in
and sits down before a large crucifix above the
main altar. All the Jews in the neighborhood
are dragged in by the soldiers to hear their
death sentence. After a mock trial they
proceed to march out of the Christian Church,
under the eyes of the soldiers of the
doublecross, as Hitler cries out: "Death to
every Jew."

Before they reach the door, the figure of
Christ on the Cross loosens His hands and
feet from the gibbet and walks in a blaze of
glory behind the last Jew, as He turns and
says to Hitler: "In that case, you will want Me
too!"

Someday we will learn that Christ is the
Savior of all men.

THE POWER OF GOD

The supreme instance of all history that the voice of the people is not necessarily the voice of God, was the moment when a mob passed beneath a cross, flinging at the helpless figure there upon it, the blistering sneer of the ages: "He trusted in God; let him now deliver him." (Matt. 27:43)

That taunt had a strong point: for how could He give life, who Himself could not master death? What added to its force was the apparent non-interference of God, which even He on the Cross acknowledged in that dereliction: "My God, my God, why hast thou forsaken me?" (Matt. 27:46)

Two days later, early in the morning, a converted prostitute is found walking in a cemetery — she whose heart has been captured by Him without, as other men had done, laying it waste. It was one of those calm dawns, suggesting the sleep of innocents and the gentle stir of angels' wings.

She was in search of a tomb and a dead body which she hoped she might anoint with spices. Arriving, she found a great stone rolled back from the rock-hewn grave, which on Good Friday had been guarded by Pilate's soldiers and the seal of which no man might break without penalty of death.

The idea of the Resurrection did not seem to enter her mind — she who herself had risen from a tomb sealed by the seven devils of sin. Finding the tomb empty she broke again into a fountain of tears.

No one who weeps ever looks upwards. With her eyes cast down as the brightness of the early sunrise swept over the dew-covered grass, she vaguely perceived someone near her, who asked: "Woman, why weepest thou?" (John 20:15)

Mary, thinking it might have been the gardener, said: "Because they have taken away my Lord; and I do not know where they have laid him. . . . Sir, if thou hast taken him hence, tell me where thou hast *laid him, and I will take him away."* (John 20:13, 15)

The figure before her spoke only one word, one name, and in a tone so sweet and ineffably tender that it could be the only unforgettable voice of the world; and that one word was: "Mary."

No one could ever say "Mary" to her as He said it. In that moment she knew Him. Dropping into the Aramaic of her mother's speech she answered but one word: "Rabboni!" "Master!" And she fell at His feet — she was always there, anointing them at a supper, standing before them at a Cross, and now kneeling before Him in the Glory of an Easter morn.

A few minutes before she was asking: "Who shall roll us back the stone?" (Mark 16:3) Now an angel clad in white is saying: "Behold the place where they laid him." (Mark 16:6)

The Cross had asked the questions; the Resurrection had answered them. The Cross had asked the question: How far can Power go in the world? The Resurrection answered: Power ends in its own destruction, for those who slew the foe lost the day.

The Cross had asked: Why does God permit evil and sin to nail Innocence and Justice to a tree? The Resurrection answered: That sin, having done its worst, might exhaust itself and thus be overcome by Love that is stronger than either sin or death.

Thus there emerges the Easter lesson that the power of evil and the chaos of any one moment can be defied and conquered, for the basis of our hope is not in any form of human power, but in the Power of God Who has given to the evil of this earth its one mortal wound — an open tomb, a gaping sepulchre, an empty grave.

If the story of Christ ended with that cry of abandonment on the Cross, then what hope have we that bruised Goodness and crucified Justice will ever rise triumphant over the massed wickedness of men?

If He Who died to give us the glorious liberty of the children of God could not break the chains of death, then what hope is there that the enslaved peoples of Europe will ever rise from the slavery of their graves to a freedom where a man can call a soul his own?

If the human power of Caesars could nail Supreme Innocence to a tree and then mingle His dust with the split rocks of a Jerusalem hillside, then what hope have we, who are far from that innocence, that we will ever master those modern Pilates who, in their vain boasts, say again: "Knowest thou not that I have power to crucify thee." (John 19:10)

If there be no Power of God that can raise to the newness of life Him Who said, "I am the light of the world," then, in brokenhearted misery must we say to our soldiers: "Out, out brief candles, there shall be no light again."

If there be no Power of God which can rescue from the ravenous wolves of death Him Who said, "I am the Good Shepherd," then let all the innocent victims of the wolves of Nazism, Fascism, and Communism throughout the world shed their tears in vain as the cold bleak earth takes the measure of their unmade graves.

If there be no Power of God to bring back to life the Physician of our souls, the Redeemer of our sins, the Teacher of our minds, then the pathos of man's mortality is deepened and the riddle of human existence darkened forever, as the prison doors of death are everlastingly shut by the Jailer whose name is Black Despair.

You say the Resurrection contradicts science and human experience; I say to you that the rotting in the grave of Supreme Truth would contradict it a thousand times more.

I can accept a universe where Goodness is crucified by Power, but I cannot accept one where there is no higher Power to raise it to justification. I can accept a world where the Church is buried in a grave, but I cannot accept a world where it stays there. I can accept a world where Evil has its hour, where a Poland is crucified between two thieves, where Jews and Christians are exiled, where the Cross is double crossed by a swastika, where 40,000 churches are closed in a land where religion is called the "opium of the people," but I cannot accept a world wherein Goodness does not have its Easter Day to sing triumphant on the wings of victory.

Thus there emerges the Easter lesson that the power of evil and the chaos of any one moment can be defied and conquered, for the basis of our hope is not in any construct of human power, but in the Power of God Who has given to the evil of this earth its one mortal wound — an open tomb, a gaping sepulchre, an empty grave.

Apply this Easter lesson to the Dark Hour in which we live. Whence shall come our hope of victory? Shall it be in the power of arms alone? Shall it be in the power of the common man alone?

Our hope for victory in this war must not be in the power of arms alone, for the enemy has the Devil on his side, and guns, planes, tanks, and shells are no match for Boasts.

As Isaiah warned: "Woe to them that go down to Egypt for help, trusting in horses, and putting their confidence in chariots, because they are many: and in horsemen, because they are very strong: and have not trusted in the Holy One of Israel, and have not sought after the Lord." (Isaiah 31:1-2)

Let the enemy come as so many armored and panoplied Goliaths thinking that steel must always be met by steel alone, and we shall, like other David's, go out to meet them unto victory clothed in the Power of Him Who gave to the evil of this earth its one mortal wound — an open tomb, a gaping sepulchre, an empty grave.

Nor, on the other hand, should our hope for a more democratic life in the world be in the common man unpurified by faith; for once in power, he will cease to be the common man unpurified by faith; for once in power, he will cease to be the common man of the proletariat and will become the uncommon man or the bureaucrat. The common man who trusts in flesh alone can be counted on to abuse his power just as much as the class he overthrew.

Rather we must trust in the common man made uncommon by the Power of Him Who dared to say to the first of all Totalitarian Caesars of Christian History: "Thou shouldst not have any power ... unless it were given thee from above." (John 19:11)

And for all of us who have the fullness of faith, be not cast down because the persecutors of religion, having laid the Church, like its Founder, in the tomb, utter the boast: "Behold the place where we laid it." Remember the law of Progress of the Church is the reverse of the law of Progress of the world.

We are most progressive when we are most hated. Since we belong to no civilization, we do not die with any civilization. If the world loved the Church, the Church would be no salvation to the world. If it were not hated, it would be weak.

It is only because the Fires of its Truth are blinding evil eyes and convicting them of sin and judgment, that they vainly try to put them out. The Church is nearest victory when it is most defeated.

And though the world is tearing up all the photographs and blueprints of a society and a family based on the moral law of God, be not disheartened. The Church has kept the negatives.

And someday they will be used again for our trust is not in human power, but in Him for Whom the tolls of execution are always sounding, though the execution never takes place.

Francis Thompson compared the Church to the lily, depicting first its defeat, then its resurrection, in these magnificent lines:

"O Lily of the King! low lies thy silver wing,
And long has been the hour of thine
unqueening;
And thy scent of Paradise on the night-wind
spills its sighs,
Nor any take the secrets of its meaning.
O Lily of the King! I speak a heavy thing,
O patience, most sorrowful of daughters!
Lo, the hour is at hand for the troubling of the
land,
And red shall be the breaking of the waters.

"Sit fast upon thy stalk, when the blast shall
with thee talk,
With the mercies of the King for thine awning;
 And the just understand that thine hour is at
hand,
Thine hour at hand with power in the
dawning.
When the nations lie in blood, and their kings
a broken brood,
Look up. O most sorrowful of daughters!

Lift up thy head and hark what sounds are in
the dark,
For His feet are coming to thee on the waters!"

(Lilium Regis)

We are living in a period of history like
unto that of the Roman Empire when Julian
the Apostate sat upon the throne of the
Caesars. The persecution of Christ which he
initiated was not like the earlier persecutions,
which were prompted by the release of a
barbaric instinct, but rather was due to the
perversion and the loss of faith in Christ. Like
his successors in the modern world, Julian
persecuted because he had lost his faith —
and since his conscience would not let him
alone, he would not let the Church alone.

There is a story to the effect that he made a
tour of the Roman Empire to investigate the
success of his persecutions. He came to the
ancient city of Antioch where, disguising
himself, he entered into the inns, taverns, and
public markets to better learn the fruits of his
hate.

On one occasion, watching thousands of
people crowd into a temple dedicated to
Mithra, he was recognized by an old Christian
friend whose name was Agathon. Pointing to
the crowd and to the apparent success of the

pagan cult, he sneered this question to his friend: "Agathon, whatever happened to that carpenter of Galilee — does he have any jobs these days?" Agathon answered: "He is building a coffin now for the Roman Empire, and for you."

Six months later Julian thrust a dagger into his own heart. Throwing it toward the heavens against which he had rebelled, as his own unredemptive blood fell back upon him, he uttered his last and most famous line: "O Galilean, Thou hast conquered!"

He always does!

ACKNOWLEDGMENTS

I want to thank Almighty God for the health of mind, body, and spirit to put together these reflections.

To my good wife, Isabel, my children, and my grandchildren, who keep me young at heart and are truly a blessing from God. Thank you for sharing in my joy.

I wish to express my gratitude to members of the Archbishop Fulton John Sheen Foundation in Peoria, Illinois — in particular, to the Most Rev. Daniel R. Jenky, C.S.C., Bishop of Peoria, for your leadership and fidelity to the cause of Sheen's canonization and the creation of this book.

To Julie Enzenberger, O.C.V., who repeated to me time and time again Sheen's words: "Believe the incredible, and you can do the impossible."

To the staff and volunteers at Sophia Institute Press for their invaluable assistance in helping to publish the writings of Archbishop Fulton J. Sheen. I am indebted to them for this great work.

To the many seminarians, priests, religious, bishops, and cardinals I have met during this journey. Always remember the words of Archbishop Sheen that "The priest is not his own."

To the tens of thousands of people I have met in my travels, giving presentations about Archbishop Fulton J. Sheen at parishes, conferences, universities, high schools, church groups, and even pubs: thank you for sharing with me your many "Sheen Stories." I truly cherish each one of them.

And lastly, to Archbishop Fulton J. Sheen, whose teachings on prayer, the sacraments, our Lord's Passion, and His Seven Last Words continue to inspire me to love God more and to appreciate the gift of the Church. His teachings and his encouragement to make a Holy Hour each day has been a true gift in my life. May I be so blessed as to imitate Archbishop Sheen's love for the saints, the sacraments, the Eucharist, and for the Mother of God. May the Good Lord grant him a very high place in Heaven!

— Al Smith

ABOUT THE AUTHOR

Fulton J. Sheen

(1895–1979)

Fulton John Sheen was born in El Paso, Illinois, in 1895. In high school, he won a three-year university scholarship, but he turned it down to pursue a vocation to the priesthood. He attended St. Viator College Seminary in Illinois and St. Paul Seminary in Minnesota. In 1919, he was ordained a priest for the Diocese of Peoria, Illinois. He earned a licentiate in sacred theology and a bachelor of canon law at the Catholic University of America and a doctorate at the Catholic University of Louvain, Belgium.

Sheen received numerous teaching offers but declined them in obedience to his bishop and became an assistant pastor in a rural parish. Having thus tested his obedience, the bishop later permitted him to teach at the Catholic University of America and at St. Edmund's College in Ware, England, where he met G. K. Chesterton, whose weekly BBC radio broadcast inspired Sheen's later NBC broadcast, The Catholic Hour (1930–1952).

In 1952, Sheen began appearing on ABC in his own series; Life Is Worth Living. Despite being given a time slot that forced him to compete with Milton Berle and Frank Sinatra, the dynamic Sheen enjoyed enormous success and in 1954 reach tens of millions of viewers, non-Catholics as well as Catholics.

When asked by Pope Pius XII how many converts he had made, Sheen responded, "Your Holiness, I have never counted them. I am always afraid if I did count them, I might think I made them, instead of the Lord."

Sheen gave annual Good Friday homilies at New York's St. Patrick's Cathedral, led numerous retreats for priests and religious, and preached at summer conferences in England.

"If you want people to stay as they are," he said, "tell them what they want to hear. If you want to improve them, tell them what they should know." This he did, not only in his preaching but also in the more than ninety books he wrote. His Peace of Soul was sixth on the New York Times best-seller list.

Sheen served as auxiliary bishop of New York (1951–1966) and as bishop of Rochester (1966–1969).

Two of his great loves were for the Blessed Mother and the Eucharist. He made a daily holy hour before the Blessed Sacrament, from which he drew strength and inspiration to preach the gospel and in the presence of which he prepared his homilies. "I beg [Christ] every day to keep me strong physically and alert mentally in order to preach His gospel and proclaim His Cross and Resurrection," he said. "I am so happy doing this that I sometimes feel that when I come to the good Lord in Heaven, I will take a few days' rest and then ask Him to allow me to come back again to this earth to do some more work."

Sheen also said that "the greatest love story of all time is contained in a tiny white host." This was the love that transformed him. His daily Eucharistic Holy Hour was legendary. From the day of his ordination to the day of his death, Sheen spent an hour a day praying in the presence of the Blessed Sacrament. From his office desk, through an open door, he could gaze upon the tabernacle at all times. His union with Christ enabled him to more fully, more accurately and more convincingly lead others to Christ in all he said and did. Sheen was a man of many talents and accomplishments, but it was Christ who enabled him to use them in the best ways.

The good Lord called Fulton Sheen home in 1979. His television broadcasts, now on tape, and his books continue his earthly work of winning souls for Christ. Sheen's cause for canonization was opened in 2002. In 2012, Pope Benedict XVI declared him "Venerable." In 2019, Pope Francis approved a miracle attributed to the intercession of the Venerable Fulton Sheen, clearing the way for his beatification.

Books Available Through Bishop Sheen Today Publishing

The Rainbow of Sorrow

The Seven Last Words

Calvary and the Mass

Love One Another

The Cross and the Beatitudes

The Cross and the Crisis

Love One Another

Victory Over Vice

The Seven Virtues

For God and Country

God and War

The Divine Verdict

God Love You

The Seven Last Words Explained

The Priest Is Not His Own

The Cross and the Crib

Philosophies at War

The Seven Last Words of Christ Explained

Father, Forgive Them for They Know Not What They Do.

This Day Thou Shall Be with Me in Paradise

Woman Behold Your Son; Behold Your Mother

My God! My God! Why Hast Thou Forsaken Me?

I Thirst

It is Finished

Father Into Your Hands I Commend My Spirit

Liberty, Equality and Fraternity

Missions and the World Crisis

Seven Words to the Cross

Seven Pillars of Peace

The Holy Hour Prayer Book

Seven Words of Jesus & Mary

www.bishopsheentoday.com